a distilled spirit

pained prose from a bar

joseph pinto

a distilled spirit

Published by Distilled Press
Printed in the United States of America

Edited by Lisa Bachhuber
Cover Design by Debbie Boettcher

www.josephpinto.com
First Edition
ISBN: 978-0-9991127-0-0 Print

for you.

the wayward

the broken

the pained

the lost

the grieving

the unloved

the lonely

the blackened

the muted

the different

the observant;

the rare.

seven pm

3. believe what you hear
4. power lunch
5. highways
6. nothing
7. the tree
8. change of seasons
9. creed
10. it's my thing, not yours
11. keyboard blues
12. the lost art of conversation
13. he's got the moves
14. empty, still you try
15. mouth
16. spectre
17. on foggy streets
18. bullshit
19. mindless
20. you
21. those eyes
22. as usual
23. mercy killing
24. hollow eyes
25. birth
26. let it out
27. dulled
28. floor mirror
29. the sweater

nine pm

eleven pm

87. not defined by your threads
88. thanks for nothing
89. your uncanny way of knowing
90. breath
91. skin and bones
92. what i learned
94. dignity
95. to carve, to own
96. it's all the same
97. crooked view
98. in this, like all else
99. and tonight you cling
100. ways of sorrow
101. keep to yourself
102. of a new age
103. childproof
104. of this i do not care
105. black
106. to take what you do not want to own
107. refill
108. a place to hang my coat
109. old fashioned love
110. attainable aspirations
111. my own god tonight
112. not yet, not ever
113. struck down
114. empty mirrors

last call

distilled

to concentrate, to purify, to obtain by distillation;
to extract the essence of life in its rawest form.

spirit

the principle of conscious being;
the soul, the heart, the seat of sentiment.

seven pm

believe what you hear

i know you heard that
i'm the resident poet
you probably think my life
has been full of heartache
missed opportunity
the occasional well-intentioned
abuse of alcohol

you're right.

power lunch

all i wished was to enjoy my scotch but
your excessive blabbering intruded on my peace.

you're the type that loves the
sound of your own voice

such an authoritative tone

yes, dignified gentleman,
your life *is* an important one;

while the declaration of your daily itinerary
seems necessary to validate your world

kindly shut the fuck up.

highways

your pain i ride
over interstates
and highways
constantly reconstructing
the scabs
routes so readily accessible
still you've no idea
the avenues i loiter
the burdens stored
on subterranean levels
shelved as i've shelved
so many others
dust laden with time.

nothing

in this dark, i am nothing

just as you see me.

the tree

her face was riddled.

dug into her cheek
an empty heart
like lovers carve into a tree.

there were no initials
no dates
just old skin

rough and crumbly like bark.

she stood alone
bowed

an ancient tree in the forest
awaiting a fall
no one would ever hear.

change of seasons

it's something how
you leave me feeling reborn
like springtime through the window
but you seem to forget
i'm allergic to pollen
sooner or later i'll wind up
longing for the frost.

creed

this is writing —
earth laden nails
grit crusted teeth
sun-scorched hide
scotch soaked pain

creed of the beast.

it's my thing, not yours

you look at me
scribbling in my pad
with a look upon your face
that says *i wonder what he's scribbling about*
i watch you
watching me
i hope you're smart enough to realize
it's none of your fucking business.

keyboard blues

she breaches
melancholy waters
only when
his fingers
pull her
back to
the surface;

until then
she drowns.

the lost art of conversation

he will never grow up
his mind still functions
in the manner of a young child
he wants to go out drinking every night
he doesn't understand
the meaning of responsibility
he gambles his paycheck away

not done, she bitches on facebook
for her friends to see
vindicated by every click of like.

he's got the moves

old man, you've got the moves
whiskey smooth

i wonder
if your raven-haired beauty
knows it's merely part
of your pitch

still you entertain her
as the candlelight flickers and
the cobwebs sway in her head.

empty, still you try

my bones gleam
my eyes ache
as your unwavering light
searches across my pores.

you curse my resolve
while you continue your
bloodletting—
when will you learn my veins dried
a long time ago.

mouth

your mouth
forever wordless
still rends a hole
you can drown me in.

spectre

in the middle of the room is a ghost
who is blind but can see what others
feel, it knows what others
have forgotten, it screams what others
don't wish to hear.

i know this ghost.

yet once i turn from the mirror
it disappears.

on foggy streets

the street lamps only know
what you want them to know
walk long enough you'll find
a new place to exist
with the same old story.

bullshit

you cannot bullshit a bullshitter
but you can buy him a drink
a few shots
get him just short of glassy-eyed
then tolerate the stream of truths
as you sort out the lesser lies.

mindless

i read the praise
the heaping of recognition
for someone who left too soon

why no thanks for a mind still creating;
why no celebration for a soul that can appreciate
your appreciation;

why wait so long
you stupid motherfuckers?

you

in a trick of light i found you
pouring venom from calloused hands
ripping faith from gibbous moon
i've loved you ever since.

your cruel grace matched by
even the coldest of gray januaries and
as the sun died
you spoke to me the foulest nothings
whispered from your alligator snout.

you poured acid in my ears to
quell my methods of thinking when
you knew full well
i had no free will at all.

chant a new song of turpitude
blasphemous act;
i'll love you ever more.

those eyes

reflected in the panes
are the pains that you mirror
and the pains that you draw
but you can never shut them out
like i could never seal you out
you are lost within yourself
as i am lost without myself
and still we gaze
and we gaze
and we gaze.

as usual

the road burns
as i burn
trying to reach you
but as usual
i'm left
spinning my wheels.

mercy killing

do you remember that day you shushed me?
silk finger on my lips stilling
my pulse
clouds fell and you
caught them, dabbed
tears from my eyes, stole the
sun's rays, stabbed them
through my heart.
mercy killing, so was whispered
still i,
i could not talk, not
with your fist down my
windpipe, sweet charm tearing
me apart.
i should have thanked you, admitted
you were never
to blame
still i,
i was the quiet one
and you,
you so insane.

hollow eyes

she has hollow eyes.

she fills them with roses
to keep away the death.

she lost her tongue
because the truth cut deep.

she is suffering's whore
but you can't afford her.

she has hollow eyes.

birth

there's beauty in pain
a sublime blackening
that is incomprehensible to
others unless
it enters the world
with you.

let it out

you're unable to suppress it
the slightest thing sends you into a tizzy
you can't see clearly
not that you could before

as tears spill from your eyes
let it out
is all i can rouse myself to say
knowing full well you'll grasp every opportunity
to let him back in.

dulled

i need to listen closely—
the pain you share
should be sharp yet
comes delivered dull, spoken
at the price of a worn tongue;

how it rends me to hear you
recall the worst of all you have been;
i sit quietly
listening to your soft grace
betrayed by the broken
fragments of your words.

i can't ever glue you back together
but i can hold you in my hands.

floor mirror

the reflection speaks lies
clay where flesh hung
wire where bones once created
sense to the structure

strength had been there
but now all is malleable
awaiting hands to reshape
to be whole again.

the sweater

i'm not quite sure what your deal is
to make things worse, you're wearing
an ugly sweater. i won't criticize your

fashion,

but i'll bury your conversation.
if i need to hear your circular
bullshit one more time, i swear

i'll douse you in scotch and light you on fire.

i can't do that, of course. i'm a civilized
man, listening to the ramblings of a brute.
at this point, i'm half-way to losing

my mind.

it's settled then. i'll spend my night with my
single malt beauty in a snifter, your pathetic
pickup lines, looking at your crappy

sweater.

delivery

it's not the words but the tone
it's not the manner but the fashion
in which your words come delivered.

nothing is ribbon wrapped
nothing is ruby pearled from your mouth.

stripping down

i don't write like you do
i don't dress up my words
like i'm taking them to broadway
i don't use frills
or pretty sequence to make them
look sparkly
emotion isn't a snowflake
it doesn't melt
it bleeds
remember that the next time you serve
vegetarian quinoa chili
while i eat my steak
emotion isn't getting dolled up for a party
it's stripping down when no one's home
you can't make a teacup yorkie
from a jackal, can you now?
i don't write like you do
i'd go fuck myself
if i did.

un

i have seen
what can't be unseen
and done
what can't be undone
while my heart has been thrown places
it can't un-be.

jumper

i admire your courage
few would see it through to completion
but you have.

i don't know what pushed you over the edge;
we all have a breaking point.

i don't know what you left behind
who am i to blame you though;
we should all be entitled a way out.

i do wonder about your new shoes however
and if you knew when you bought them
that you'd be leaving them behind.

a spider matters

if you listen closely enough
you can hear the light bulb's hum
it doesn't do you any favors
as you inspect your face of sin
earthquake fissures
yes it gives them all away
no amount of cream will help
you're fucked
the way a spider is fucked
when you throw it in the toilet
flush it
watch it spin for eternity;
the spider's eternity.

scrub
or scour
it makes no difference
take a good look at your skin
prepare for the next seismic event
listen closely to the light bulb's hum
tell yourself you're not responsible
for anything
not even as the spider
screams.

ode

i drank you in a coffeehouse
but i wrote you in a bar.

under the gun

a crafted hand
eviscerates
shreds skin into bloody ribbons
speaks my story so precisely
i wish to scream
no more

my tale starts anew
another chapter splits open;
the truth of me
served raw.

deep thaw

and yet i weep as the frost plucks my lash;
tempest—
i will never be reborn come spring.

ashes

i praise you
but do not wear your mark
my soul is darkened; neither of us doubt it

can you appreciate the realness of me?

no amount of supplication will spare me these deeds
and we know it;

my sins not yours to bare.

the master craftsman

she crafts three masks
deaf dumb blind
with a clumsy hand
that only speaks more decisively
for lack of authenticity.

i try to advise her
but she cannot hear
just like my reasoning is beyond her.

before her sightless eyes
i have passed the truth
countless times;

she is a sad example
of love gone wrong
but it hasn't stopped me
from molding a face all my own.

perils of greasy calamari

he didn't so much kiss her from across the bar
than he devoured her face;
the calamari i'd just eaten
tasting even greasier on my tongue.

i swear if he kissed her one more time
i'd push my fingers down my throat.

nine pm

gentleman johnnie

johnnie
you're back in black and
isn't it fitting we sit here again
conversation smooth as ever
a welcome reprieve

the longer we sit
the more i'll indulge
ever stoic
you never judge

you never turn away
listening

as i share silent heartbreak
choices hindered
dreams asunder

but you won't stray far
will you, dear johnnie?

you bring calm to the storm
still the fire in my veins
until these burdens
fade to blurry edges
the pain a bit dulled;

43

a welcome reprieve.

thank you, johnnie
together we are back in black

selfless gentleman
always knowing what i need.

spoiled

ringed round her martini glass she left her angry mouth
still incomplete with thoughts half ingested
like the food wasting in her dish
his words by now long grown spoiled.

just not here

on this darkened night i hold you
arms empty
your memory my solitary light
wind raps at the pane
sneaks under the door
the only thing ever to cross this threshold again
sandwich on the counter grows stale with mold
milk sour
spoiled

none of it matters; this candle flickers
ghosts, they creep along the floor
sounding so much the way your footfalls once did
when you kissed my cheek standing in the hall.

i'd walk somewhere if it wasn't raining so hard
these clothes already stuck to my skin
the weight of everything
the wait for anything.

i'll sit here then
because somewhere, you are there
somewhere, just not here.

on this darkened night i hold you
somewhere
just not here.

fog

i will allow the fog to birth me
obscure my definition
in swirls of grey shrouded whispers
when you wish to know me,
i will be gone.

hand poised on knob

you've had your bags packed
for a very long time,
no chance to think it over
just grabbed your essentials
essentially, you're already gone

but still you remain
for what or why
you're not sure yourself
and that's the problem, isn't it

remaining behind the door
hand on knob
certain of the monster behind you
not sure of the monsters beyond

duffel bag on your back
mouth dry as cotton
frozen in place
so you remain another day;
but your bags are packed
in your head you're gone
living your life this way
one day at a time

one monster clawing at your back;
god knows what waiting beyond.

spawn

this, this place...

where first i laid eyes on you
beckoning from atop the crest.

i would rip gods from the skies
to be with you.

i fight the currents;
i swallow deeply our acheron
its vile taste leaves me reborn.

thunder in my ears
cascading veil 'cross my eyes;
i cannot refuse you
how i relish the way you bloat me.

let me swirl
detritus amidst your feet.

allow me rest for a moment;
the gravel bed serves me well.

speak of my sacrifice at the headwaters
slice free from me my spawn.

pseudo cerulean queen

pseudo cerulean queen, i can see the storm
come loping across your eyes,
your darkness a dead giveaway that
the only thing blue about you is your soul

drench me in sorrow;
open the deluge of your being

i wish to reach out, cup your pain,
feel it dribble from between my fingers

as the puddle at my feet grows,
i watch your reflection shimmer,

the lightning above dividing us always.

desecrate

tone deaf to my screams
your only wish
to desecrate my whispers.

gallon of milk

on the way out
of the convenience store
i passed the magazine rack
something made me pause
a title

find your way to god

i turned
beside me
a tired woman
in crusty pants
weathered shoes
in better condition than her face.

she was desperate to find faith
in the pack of smokes
she was buying

and i was sure she carried
more heartbreak
than pennies in her pocket.

i'd heard of pennies from heaven
but those gates had closed on this woman
a long time ago and
i realized,

walking out with my gallon of milk,
that god did not wish to be found.

the unseeable

i cherish this darkness i fell into
i see what would otherwise be unseeable
the truth where once i had been blind
you never have understood
i accept that peace at last
yet do not confuse it for forgiveness;

i draw closer to the long pull of shadow
sanctuary to the gospel you peddle.

unrisen

they say jesus christ rose
and walked among the living

you weren't there
but you believe it

yet you have no faith
i'll ever make something of myself.

your debt

purse your lips
pinch your mind
toss memories
like unwanted coins

a quarter short of a buck
but no one notices
the constant reminder your own
of the price fashioned to pay

you wish this debt
to the ferryman settled
instead you fight the current
of a conscious darkened stream

you dream of sinking
with silver lined pockets
but you've no change left
to spare.

complete

i'll take what's left of you
and reassemble your pieces
no need for glue
no use for twine
for you're perfect broken
shattered
pieces long gone.

i'll lay you across the table,
my jigsaw
the sum of your parts
telling a story
filled with gaping holes
that make perfect sense
only for me.

american bbq

pick a time
does two sound good?
sure, you'll bust a nut
suffer through the day

someone takes your favorite chair
doesn't ask why you're standing
raves about their job
not noticing that you breathe air

they drink your favorite beer
ask for cheese on their burger
sorry, yours is raw?
don't worry, the cook's already there

the american barbecue
when it's all over
you keep the burners on high
so you can sear your soul atop the grill.

heard

silence;
a river runs through my head; train
brakes screech in the distance
its solace muffled
much the way i am—
unable to find my tongue.

fog clouds
the windows; it's unbearable
the droplets streaking the glass expose
highways, crossroads the likes of which
i'll never have the nerve to explore.

still in my head i trace a
route so blissfully appealing
compared to the silence
flooding my ears;

the loudest thing i'll ever hear.

resolutions

it's how it goes
raise a glass
or a paper cup
be gluttonous and gorge

worry about the calories
when you join the gym that
you'll turn your back on
a month down the road

but your resolution
won't last nearly that long

a grand idea now
it glitters like the
ornaments on your tree
soon to be packed away

forgotten and cold in your attic
boxed from the cruelties of winter
still by summer they'll remain

like your gym membership
a grand idea

awaiting the polish of a new year.

the room you live in

little girl
so lost
so forlorn
the room you live in holds cracks that
will only widen with time
your skin as translucent
as the lies you tell yourself—

this is the way it's supposed to be.

you wait
till your eyes pale
and the paint flakes from the walls.

high time

you've squandered so much
your eyes are worn
staring at lost opportunity
staring at the brittle glass that holds
the sand you can't keep from draining
between your fingers
it may be high time
to count your losses
move on.

boarding pass

he's not coming back
i think you know that
as your coffee colds
the sugar lumps
and the well-to-do's
grow stale in your mouth
he's a continent away
but only a half-mile from your house
the runway so much longer than you thought
the departure quicker than you'd like.

fruitless driving

your mind exists in a hidebound world of one-way
streets
and cul de sacs;
there are no yield signs, there are no stops.

it is an ugly place, every dead end looking like
the last.

nothing

nothing will stand between us;
nothing will keep me away
the cruelty, locked in your silent world
all you hear is nothing, even as i shout your name
what see of you beyond the reflection of spirit-churned
skies
what know of you within that haunted heart
i shall shatter your glass; recover your incarcerated soul
the cruelty, shackled in your listless words
all you think is nothing, even as i cry your name
what suffer of you behind bricked walls
you wait eternally; i say wait no more.
nothing will deny sky from its horizon
angels of their fall

nothing.

somber reminders

granite monolith; you offer me no solace

i should know by now that your
grey skinned callousness will rob these flowers
of their hue. i must look to you
to provide artificial protection; i
loathe it. lightning cracks; although
shadows dance, you still have no life.
forever you mark these grounds

i couldn't forget your way if i tried.

parapraxis

i misheard you when you misspoke
a rare moment of clarity
that made the world seem right

you knew i was a sucker for lies
an addict to false idols.

radio

she opened her soul
on the radio.

i heard her crack through
the crackle of static
wondered how nice it must be
to ache in anonymity

to slice a vein
allow the faceless
to hear you dwindling.

she feared she had lost her man.

i didn't have the heart to call in
and tell her she was right.

down the drain

you've lost her
to another year
to another remedy
to another casual outburst
of regrets. it's so much
a disease of which
there is no cure
spreading and multiplying
breaking you down into
molecules, more insignificant
than you'd ever thought
could be possible. anything
is possible with love
but you don't have love
so it's really all for naught,
isn't it?

simple shift

the sun disguises everything
just a simple shift in minutes
hides the streaks on the pane
dirt on the glass
view from without;

from within
the scene is as it ever was
only more appealing
when the shades are drawn.

no revision

damn her,
he wanted to write;

he bled instead
smudging pages
blurring thoughts
gashing every line
with a question mark.

going nowhere

look at you
pedaling so fiercely
going somewhere
nowhere

obituary in your sweaty palms
from your brow drops
tombstones crafted of salt
and the inevitable.

threads

it's not the waiting that kills me
but the lingering
she says.

she looks so pretty in her blossom dress
so lost.

she cups her hands and prays
for godless comfort;

it appeases me more than it does her.

i try to ease her across the threshold;
she slams the door closed.

don't
it's the lingering;
it's the only thing we have left.

73

above

i am desperate
for a storm to breathe new life
under these wings of mine
so that i may soar
not flutter
as i always do against this grey sky;
for once i wish to see
what i've risen above
instead of dreaming
of the promise i've left behind.

time worn

your heart is time worn
only when sifting through dust
do i discover your complexity
you have lived a hundred years in shambles
painting pictures on your walls.

with your blessing
i'll break myself deciphering you
even knowing you're meant to be unsolved.

funny what you believe

she won't ever see you as you are
just like she won't ever love you
as you'll be.

some things are beyond comprehension:
child prodigies
life after death
the possibility of world peace

sadly in all this
she believes.

loose words

he's not coming;
you dab the
makeup at your eye.

your head spins
with his loose words;
the truth harder to swallow
than his lies.

no help

remove the crucifix
find it knotted

how little you know
yet you know all there is
of unraveling

you have never learned
to undo your own knots

leave it
your crucifix
where you laid it down

you wish for no help
from anyone
or any god.

winter's sunset

there's nothing i can hide
under this winter's sunset
wind grates your name
across my cheek
swallows words that no longer
hold any warmth

yet i live for the moment
my long shadow will meld
with yours
under this pastel gloom.

night awakens and steals
you once again
leaving me with nothing

but my reimagining of the
seasons; the wind carrying
a name turned to frost on my lips.

native son

his native land etched in his
eyes
its dirt still worn into his
skin
his knuckles swollen with
hurt

he won't ever tell you
he won't ever let on

he's got his heart on a shelf back
home
it's full of love, not quite so
cold
as the cold this life has delivered
him

he won't ever cry
no
he won't ever let
go

he'll smile, order another bourbon
he'll smile, order another lie.

she walks

she walks with summer's
swoon, breeze at her back
regal considerations always
on her mind.

you would certainly fall in
line behind her, mesmerized
by the cadence of her stilettos alone;
alone, she walks.

she rips the
cigarette from her mouth and
crushes it
against the sidewalk.

a red stain from an unloved mouth.

wick

to twist
to dance
to sway
to catch your smile
in gilded embrace

to live
knowing your breath alone
will extinguish my existence.

redundancy

you've come to drown in redundancy
impale yourself on straws
your napkin bears the print of a sticky hand
much cleaner than yours

the rings upon the bar
mark a moment
a reason
a time

when you lost yourself in losing
a life that was never yours.

tuesday night at the pub

from here
i see everything
nuance, twitch, inflection.

i sit merely to observe
watch, study, comprehend.

i feel everything
life, love, loss.

your entire world now mine.

i'm here every tuesday night
feeding off your pain

as i slowly sip my scotch.

eleven pm

not defined by threads

your suit demanded an audience before you did
its sophistication clearing a path before you
the way your jet-black hair streaked backward
from your high brow
only lent to the belief we commoners did not belong
in the same room as you

even your mustache claimed a higher tax bracket.

i did not expect to find you in the men's room
as i rinsed spicy chorizo from my fingertips;

i did not expect you to piss all over the urinal
leave without washing your hands.

motherfucker.

thanks for nothing

i'm appreciative of your compassion;
ice cube cold but not quite as neat as
the scotch waiting before me

it will serve to warm me just fine—
thanks for nothing;
i know that's hard for you to understand

a foreign concept; not the understanding
but the simple thanks; perhaps you
should resort to drinking the hard stuff.

it'll make you say things i'm sure
you would never mean.

your uncanny way of knowing

how sad, you told me,
your eyes no longer dance
the symphonies you
used to orchestrate no longer
echo in your head
and yet, you told me,
i can hear you scream in the
silence, the chords you once struck
for the living
now a hymn for the dead.

breath

the loudest words are the softest spoken
you said into a paper bag.

i held it for safe keeping
watching your chest rise
so shallow
so slow.

soon you departed;

your words now fill my ear
one captured breath at a time.

skin and bones

all this time i thought i'd hidden the cancer
from my skin
never realizing it had eaten me throughout
you noticed i was much emptier than i'd ever been
still you loved me in my metastasized state.

what i learned

listen

i drink too much
say too little
trip over my words
more times than not

i'm a wreck
carefully crafted of
dough and
papier-mâché

i doubt myself
believe in concealed things
my faith gets me from bed
in the morning

i like my cereal soggy
enjoy a snack late at night
when my eyes seem lost
it's entirely intentional

i'm a hard worker
i fail even greater;
tell me why karma hasn't bitten
everyone else in the ass;

i measure mortality in
scotch buzzes
my days removed from school;
they teach you everything there

but fail to learn you about yourself.

dignity

dignity
only means something to you
once it's taken
like an old charm
gone from your breast.

to carve, to own

slave to my existence
i have you bound
tethered
wrist to foot
dance, puppet
rejoice in life i grant
at jerk of string;
obedient one
i whittle your very being
at my discretion.

it's all the same

your face is saurian
eyes slanted,
weighted by
misnomers;

you craft a good game
for the sympathetic ear,
you are not
who you say you are;

chameleon
charlatan
it's all the same
i know you

still, you are a stranger.

crooked view

life is full of
missed absolution
wasted opportunity
that weighs us down
with doubt
like failing to straighten
a crooked sin nailed to the wall;

i never seemed to mind
the cracks running through
my own walls;

i have photographs hung there
none were store bought
i could tell you what all of them mean.

in this, like all else

you've no need for my broken bones
my unsung songs
no sense of my sensibility
like everything else
you've no clue.

and tonight you cling

strive for attention
spend a small fortune on those nails
that scratch along weary shoulders
gone too long from home
still this is where you belong
with the empty faces
the weighted words
sometimes they'll buy you a drink
the way a treat might be dropped
for a wayward dog
your self-respect has fled short
of happy hour's calling;

you search those faces
you cling to those fleeting words.

ways of sorrow

there's no mourning
no pain
the dirt fills the hole
before the memories are pissed
out in the morn
dulling the recollection
by the eve's next pour.

keep to yourself

you're watching me wield my pen
as if i'm about to plunge it into your neck
and i certainly may
but your heart will suffice nicely;

i'll extract secrets
by poking deep with this ballpoint
but your sins,
your sins are what i truly want
they'll fill my pages neatly—

i've a penchant for smudged words.

of a new age

we are all as one
she said;
the great wheelwork spun behind her eyes.

it bore into me
that horrible flaking of rust
the anguished drumming of the mechanism she was.

still, i would have followed her anywhere.

into the mouth of the machine, she said—
yes, into the mouth of madness.

i cuffed my sleeves and exhaled
watching her shudder like an awakening beast
as she gathered steam.

she was right
we are all as one;
i closed my eyes and finally surrendered.

extending my hand
she took me
shorn me as she had been shorn.

childproof

wrap the corners
protect yourself; they always
find ways around the barrier

a chord struck each time
mouths twist;
you feel toddler small

spanked by left-handed lessons
of obedience; chest heaving
with perpetual sobs.

of this i do not care

speak to me your most private and secret of things;

i will be deaf to them.

share with me your every fold and deepest of chasms;

i will leave you to them.

indulge me of your every whim and fascination;

i will curse you to them.

black

i lay in bed most every night
staring into the dark
the wine on my nightstand
black in its glass

i feel for it carefully
always afraid i'll spill it
stain the sheets

somehow it hammers down my throat
bright red and angry;
a good vintage

but i wonder
if the person drinking it
is bad

the similarities are startling—
my life and this wine

i don't give it time to breathe
nor do i give a damn

staring into the shadows
i'm safe in the knowledge
that after another glass
my mind will go black as well.

to take what you do not want to own

this box no longer yours
becomes a useful place
for all the things
that once remained of you

eviscerated
stripped clean to bone
once corporeal
now just memory
upon another's exhale.

the compartments you govern
belong in potter's field
frivolous as the things
that still burden you with need

if only my soul a warehouse
you could store
all your needless, needless boxes
and rid yourself of its waste.

if only i could free you
of your needless, needless boxes
make them mine
this box no longer yours.

refill

your exhale
measured carefully
pours into your glass.

i can drink your pain
if i have to
but it would leave me
wanting a refill.

a place to hang my coat

old aches follow me in
new ones too
throb in my back greets me
the way my dog once did
i can't shake this so easily
i can't hang it upon the hook
like my coat.

old man winter comes knocking
but my bones
my bones are no longer home.

old fashioned love

he fell into her
the way a drunk falls
into his bottle
head first
care free
heart drowning in memories
of last call.

attainable aspirations

if i drink myself to death
at least i will have achieved something.

my own god tonight

fogged i am, and still i cannot clear
my reflection from what i perceive
in my mind. the water is as cleansing
as the voices in my head;
if you stop and listen closely, you
will hear them too, beckoning
to the infinite ends. still, i pause
to recollect myself, lather and
reconnect myself—
i cannot dig this razor into my cheek hard
enough. my grief, like my stubble,
falls, only to grow back thicker by tomorrow's end.
fogged, and still this steam cannot obscure
what i trick myself to comprehend.

on and on these voices beckon:
you are your own god tonight.

not yet, not ever

use my words against me

keeper of the tomes
only you've collected

try as you might
you will never become
my teacher.

struck down

i am struck as you strike
you remain my only companion
when the boughs go barren;
i feel them scoring my bones.

one day i will be dust
i will be gone;
as you strike
i will be struck down.

you mark my time
keeping my passage
through the lonely
cold days.

empty mirrors

the mirror holds your soul
while you impale your morals
beneath high heels
you move in ways god never intended
ways only a man could appreciate.

you curse the benjamins
that steep in tepid spills
across the bar
yet still you've grown used to their
sticky fingered touch wetting your skin
if only the dj could hear you cracking;
the sound of diamond ambitions crushed

much like that of the weeping
of your parents' hearts.

scored

this callus you'll never
soften; hardened
beyond my years
stripped of my pretense;
you found me in this skeletal state
scored to the bone.

bylines

they see fit doing what they
want when they
want, discrediting the
bylines that had been meticulously
arranged;

story by story
they've become old news and
this masked collage just isn't
something you want taped to
the wall any more.

boy on strings

my last january breath rose in a plume to the sky
and left me wondering if this would be how
my soul would one day escape me.

wispy vapored, twanged by fingers of northeast wind,
i suppose i will always be a puppet but the excuse
of *it will be much warmer tomorrow* keeps me
from cutting the fishing wire.

i love the dangling, but if you should ask me i
will vehemently deny it, blow frozen curses into your
face then request that you reposition me.

a light snow falls; february knocks and soon all trace
of my existence will vanish from the air. still, i will
always dangle here, waiting for your hand to guide me.

oceans

the sheets welcomed her
wrapped her limbs
drew her under their surface.

her nights are nothing
but oceans of
deep rooted sighs now;

every exhalation more telling than the last.

devour

the exhalation is birthed.

and in the night
hands strike
the passage of time.

breaths become
pained manifestations;
no one notices.

bodies sleep on pins and needles;
bodies sleep with rolling eyes
while tendrils of rancor

devour worlds.

no apologies

spare me your frilly phrases
you paint daffodils upon your soul
you're out of touch with reality
i will nail your heart to the wall.

mold

she saw him there;
in the half-light of candle
he seemed a flickering wraith
but the scorching expression with which
he regarded her only served to extinguish
her further.

she wished to reach out,
to reshape the face she once recognized,
but clay will only harden if left to serve as
testament to time.

the offing

the offing you became
dark and somber;
perpetually turbulent
those eyes

yet i cast myself
to your blackened waters;
life you delivered
death into my lungs.

look at you

look at you;
so smug in a chiseled suit
dagger tie
you speak of perry ellis
in a raised hush
as if this tone will cast
your nobility across the walls
bask in the admiration of
commoners
behind your dark rimmed
frames;
little know you that to the ferryman
i have already paid my dues;
you can shed your designer fabrics
but i remain clad always—
bone and sweat and fire.

scourge of my garden

it was cold
winter cold
you were nearly dead
but not quite
i wish i'd just left you
where i found you
instead i took you home
now you bloom
beneath a new sun
there's nothing i can do
to root you.

the seat beside me

sporting a black eye,
he tells me:

*women are like booze
but you can't get punched in the face
for sucking on the neck of a bourbon*;

his voice slurs with decades of bad decisions;
his eyes swim like
confused fish in a dirty bowl.

i watch him drink
until those fish go belly-up
then order myself another scotch.

reprieve

is it okay if i lay beside you?
because i can't keep my eyes open much longer
i've been pretty tired as of late
and things have seemed to slow down around me.

is it okay if i cry on your pillow?
i'd wash it but it'll dry soon enough
that's the way an old ache goes
flowing with the deep thaw
soon parched from summer's haze.

is it okay if i call out old names in the dark?
the more i speak them the more i'll remember not to
forget
i'd like to write them in a jazz song someday
sing a melody whether the band's ready or not.

is it okay if i lay beside you?
won't be much longer till i see the light
and that old ache flows on

whisper to me while my breaths grow shallow
whisper to me goodnight.

longed for

in the end they fucked me over
the angels the gods, they fucked me all

mostly the angels
who were tasked to watch over me
protect and provide for me

i grew my own crop and
pissed them off when i
harvested my own soul

what did they expect

they called it free will
i called it rebellion
and they wept as i danced

they branded me with stigma as i
marked the sly curl of their lips—
they longed for this life they
cursed me to all the while.

second hand smoke

he drew smoke from his cigarette
then drew smoke from my mind
walls stark that surrounded him
he stared straight ahead
puckered his lips;
dragged

*"i was like you
once, i cared."*

i was struck by the definition
of his chiseled cheekbones.

i couldn't help but inhale
his grievance.

soon i fell in line;
sallow skinned
cut from a clean cloth
together we stared forward
saying nothing
while i pondered my identity.

in the last dusty bar

i thought i'd lost it
it had been so long
since i felt anywhere near right
it found me in the
last dusty bar
sauntered beside me
spurned my questions
splashed scotch across my
lips
lit fire to my
tongue
and said:
write, motherfucker.

my muse has a way with words.

last call

wings and a prayer

i finish my hot wings
go to the bathroom
wet my hands;
there's no soap.

like so much else in my life
i start clean only to be left
a mess.

i return to my seat
drink my scotch
with dirty fingers
wishing i had the just right amount of towels
to wipe my slate clean.

fakes need not apply

the thing about this mask
is that i choose not to wear it
i'm comfortable

exposed

without this mask
you see me for all i am
so shame on you
for not seeing me coming

but you and your kind
you wear the masks i choose not to
you wear the masks i see through
a brilliant disguise?

spare me

i walk raw
naked and senses alive
even while the rest of me dies

just do me this favor
only this one

when i'm gone
display this mask alongside my casket—

to serve as a constant reminder
for the fakes who need not attend.

weed

ye who plants the seed shall burden the responsibility
of the fruit, yet suffer the toil of a heart laden with dirt.

grown useless, gnarled, twisted now under the rising
gale of wind;
a storm that shall never cease.

how one craves for the roots to be severed
yet still holds fast, reaching for the light;

a spot of sunshine that forever evades the touch.

prayers make me a killer

there's no good reason why you're still alive
another of god's cruel tricks — a glimpse
of the miracle known as the human spirit

yes, yes, miracles
if they existed you wouldn't be
in this shit hole

what point is there melting into sheets
melding into subconscious minds that
still clutch to the notion that life is kind

i pray he strikes you down; call me murderer
i demand your freedom from this cesspool
your right to find dignity at last.

immurement

and now there is nothing, nor shall there ever be;
from light i have walled myself, immurement eternal;
so shall i become one with stone. my fortress,
my penitentiary—a fitting fate; obscurity wrapped
as melded shawl round my shoulders.
yet still you find your way, flitting 'tween cracks
i believed mortared so long ago.
ivy seeks my companionship; so too do you seek
to entwine my heart. i have grown unjustly hardened,
so wrongly decayed. leave me, do you hear?
i deserve as much. let me solidify as i contemplate
the ways i have erred, gone wrong.

knock, do i

knock, do i
upon the door of death
forbidden, my release.

knock, do i
my tears marbleize
harder than your empathy.

knock, do i
the echo maddening
refused still, my entry.

at midnight

this vein opened at midnight
bloodletting like the bottle i have drunk
but i am not
drunk that is
rather in a state of noise

the creak of stairs betrays my lonely descent
betrays the descent i have long disguised

i am done with this
this life
this rage, this sorrow;
it is a perpetual pain of self
a totality i cannot escape

yet i usher in another midnight
another bloodletting
another restless night no different
than the last.

husk

the call came
you were gone
all that remained
was the simple act of driving
to see you one last time.

you left the party
long before last call
too soon
after the final hello.

your own terms
abided always;
something i admire.

you left me
a husk
something you never were
something hard to erase from memory
always unforgiving.

during that simple act of driving
when all that remained
were your terms
i remembered the final time i lay with you
a husk;

the party long over
the curtain long drawn.

tattletales

it was much easier to tell where i was going
than explain where i had been
my narration evolving
the further away i walked

that was the beauty of it;
into the flush gloam i stepped
as easily as i stepped into my shoes
aware that found things often provide
a natural fit

i doubt i shall ever look back
i will go where the going takes me,
the sun and the boughs and the
tattletale crows over my shoulder.

flattened

like the words written
i go unseen
imploring from lips equally ignored
flattened
compressed to fit into a one-dimensional world
not even worthy of rose-colored glasses
the grey wash that stains me slowly fading

the torrents before unnoticed
the slightest breeze now leads me astray
you haven't the sense to figure
the smile taped to my face
is the crumpled one from yesterday.

yesterday's fable

was it just yesterday you told me your time had come?
under a cloudless sky
nothing but myth and unspoken promise between us;
it was an alabaster lie.

i realize as much now
but i was so blind to my own beliefs
that i forgot to realize
my faith belongs
only to borrowed time.

it still hangs in the air
of that cloudless sky
so fleeting when spoken
so final when remembered:

i might not be here tomorrow
i might not see you again.

i laughed, not at you, of course
but at your absurdity
something i steadfastly refused to own.

but with today's cloudless sky born new
and yesterday's fable yet grown old
i realize how shabby these beliefs are in my pocket
and you've forced me to throw them all away.

145

wrong frequency

they don't hear me cry out
it takes a great deal of patience to dial in silence
they're on the wrong frequency
the waves i emit bounce off nothing.

i'm alone in this vacuum
it expands by the day.

don't confuse the issue; i'm used to the solitude
it's the exclusion that wears me out.

moving on

fuck you—

she destroyed the effigy
she'd carefully crafted
for so many years

drove a chisel through the fine
features she'd memorized
under her fingertips
hammered pristine pieces
into infinite dust.

where'd i go wrong—
she wondered
took to her latest creation
in clay.

savior

man made of steel
why won't you come down from
your perch high above this metropolis

save me.

i've desperately tried to fly in your cape
but you left me no field guide;
in this world i need to be more than just
a hero.

do you remember when
i gazed upon you with wonder
an unflinching conviction that you were no
mere mortal…

please can't you see
how hard i struggle to soar
i've no air with which to take flight.

a cry;
i dash

carrying this life in my arms
shielding her from life's evils
forever her guardian
her imperfect savior;

148

to the skies i look
searching for mine.

by fingertips

call to me
seduce me with a whispered promise
of release

carried upon the streams of amber goodness
and white pebbled paths of grandeur;

is your song of lullabied silence
merely a fable?

as i grow dulled
how i long for you to claim me
remove me of my daily climb
from this darkened abyss;

no longer would my pain
define me.

infinite sadness

i was born
with an infinite sadness
that has resonated
since the womb
and has held my hand
down every corridor of my life
and i do not know why

i do not know why

i was born
with an infinite sadness
that has defined me
since a child
on my happiest days
and in my merrier moments
it has held me down
and i do not know why

i do not know why

i was born
with an infinite sadness
that i can taste
as i taste blood
and heavy is its weight
upon my shoulders;

my burden alone to bear
and i do not know why

i do not know why.

atomic number 26

still you've no understanding of
my stories lost before you
words stripped of their most basic composition
left to crumble in a fitting tribute of oxidation

you'll always view me that way
nothing more than your atomic number 26
while the greater part of me
flakes bit by bit over time

i mourn the days
when my message rang true;
beauty gleamed through my imperfection

now i go unnoticed, a broken tale;
a gate through which nothing can ever pass again
such a wasted thing
left here

your tainted breath corrupting
every last line of my expression.

onward, my son

i understand now

your need to die alone
as the heaping shovels of dirt i threw
have only come back
to choke my throat

the purge of sins—

you kept your poker hot
while i, cold
desiring the kiss of dull blade
and a heavy-handed demise

i've always been in your eyes
were you willing to blink me away?

or did you know i'd follow in your steps
the apple never falling far from the tree

look at me
am i what you were?
am i what you wished to be?
or altogether worse?

you sent me away—

i understand now
because in that grand heart of yours
you could never be still
as i can never stay whole

and as i choke on dirt and pick at the scab of sins
i go on as you sent me
never more alone.

truth lies

the light streams beautifully
through your translucent nature
your words billowing like feathers
lost in flight
yet unabashed in its nakedness
the truth lies

and lies
in sedimentary foundations.

dried glue

your frown seems longer in the shadows
your eyes flutter like autumn leaves
seeking solace in the breeze

between us the empty shell of something once we'd
born
my fingers so clumsy
trying to glue it back

laughter fades in the rearview
a ghost of broken promise all that remains in the street

it's okay, we'll talk, won't we?
of times when air rushed through our hair
the open road a cherished child
we played favorites, didn't we?
always the same marker until we reached a place our
own

but today your eyes signal a storm on the horizon
your lips flutter like autumn leaves
seeking compassion along with the breeze

we held that empty shell of something once, didn't we?
my fingers ever so clumsy
trying to glue it back.

social media

how you bask in your wasteland of
keeping with the jones'
your throne beset of lavish rhetoric

ironically not of your voice
so desperate for approval you are;
lost puppet

you simply manage the content
the slant
while you dangle and jerk from strings

i await the day you announce
your monumental failings with the same zeal
we both know that will never happen

your fertile womb births prejudices, opinions
that should have been aborted upon inception
king to your keyboard;

a fool surrounded by jokers upon the screen.

flinch

the worst of me is reflected
every time you flinch
i can't explain how it tears me apart
the darkening of your twinkling eyes
cloudy with confusion
pleading with something
beyond your understanding
i was you once—
so how can i explain
i've seen that reflection before
a beast you should never have to glimpse
yet it exists
a foul mannered thing.

scotch drinker's lament

you agree with me as often
as that cheap scotch did
and your bite
just as bad—
i wish i never had to swallow either of you.

no amount of cubes
will ever water you down
so i am forced to tolerate
the angry buzz inside my head
while discount moments go on without end.

worse still, quite unlike
the premium labels i now drink
nothing about us
will ever be neat.

burn to your core

still i survive here
i am charred;
i am lifeless
without ever having died.

you surround me with portrait skies
my limbs can never touch;
only the water to nourish me
delivered by beak of bird
sob of storm.

yes, you planted me in barren ground
but i chose to take root
strove to blossom.

more than ever, i realize i cannot.

how deathly i must appear
against the backdrop you manufactured
an obstruction to all you'd thought perfected
an eyesore so startling i am beauty in my own right.

it must burn to your core.

bowed still i stride

the universe seems hell-bent on diminishing me;
storms may reshape my landscape but
i refuse to seek higher ground

i will not compartmentalize to fit any ideal but my own;
bowed still i stride as the fates hit hurricane pitch,
i will know i lived free of compromise after all.

gone

i think the only reason i'm sitting
in this bar
is because there is a part of me that believes
you'll still walk through the door
and perhaps you will;

i imagine you
at the opposite end,
a stack of bills before you
a solid three finger pour in your hand

the bartender saunters over
places an upside-down shot glass in front of me
from the gentleman, she says
nodding in your direction

but when i glance, you aren't there

the ghost of you will stay with me forever
long after the buzz of our scotch is gone.

a final toast with death

i await you
my bravado more resolute than ever
this snifter in my hand unwavering
these drops of scotch delivered faithfully to my lips
so come to me, sir reaper
you whose work is never done

you've stolen a good man from this world
left behind his only son
i have no fear of you this day
not while my veins run hot,
coward!

a good man seeks retribution
his weapon his only son
i await you
be a gentleman
share this final scotch
drink with me, sir reaper

i have work not nearly done.

guilt of a meal

he cut the cloth quite reluctantly but so
plastic fake
whiskey thin for the length of time i remained.
his son came to me, stubble oddly more
worn than his eyes.

told me: *he looks great, doesn't he?*
but he'd roll over if he knew i'd dusted off that
old suit. he was always so comfortable wearing
hand me downs. i smiled
not so comfortable in my stuffy coat, thinking
the heat must be cranked
to hide the coolness of the corpse.

i did all i could; said farewell
feeling i'd not done enough, then later
ordered prime rib, a craft beer,
all while he remained unmoving, uneating and
uncommonly dressed.

by definition

you don't get me;
you read my words
they come delivered in a
magniloquent fashion
you don't comprehend

look it up, it means
speaking in a lofty,
grandiose style

the joke of it all
is that you see me
as a commoner
a jester;
the pauper

you don't get me;
no matter the dictionary
in your hands
you'll never fathom the intent
of my heart.

tired of walking

it's too late to save me
i've already committed suicide
just not the kind you can wrap
a shroud around

spared you the mess
spared you the noose round rafter
by the time you figure me out
my ghost will have preceded me
by miles.

vigil

how many times must i light
this candle, only to glimpse your
ghost flit and cavort through
the flame

how many times must i burn my
fingers in loving memory, only to have
the sting of burning flesh remind me
that you are gone.

no mercy

chill in my bones
birthed from footfalls across my grave

ringing in my ears
spawned by whispers ill intent

my conscious stripped clean
i will strike you down

drive you to your knees
laugh as you have laughed
watching me stumble all my years.

never trust anyone

i have a bird
that nestles its head
between my fingers
chirps until i pet it
until i gently scratch under its wings
rub its beak
what a sight, this bird
what a cute little character
god's handiwork on display.

i doubt anyone could say
upon watching its public display
that it lacks a soul
that it lacks a motivation to love
as it nestles its head
between my thick fingers
so trusting of the human condition
i realize how easy it would be
to snap its tiny neck.

at the root of it

at the root of it
i think i am going to die
an unhappy man
cherished memories to hold onto
moments i will bring with me into the light
yet i believe i will go weeping
unable to let go of that which i could not grasp
not the way i wanted to
replaying the failures far more
than the greatest successes of my life.

why is it not me

i loathe every day
for bringing her
into a world beyond control.

she is as lost as
i have never been found.

why must i watch her suffer
why is it not me
why is it not me?

she loves me
but i cannot love myself.

a distilled spirit

you perpetually refuse
to accept me for me
seeking instead to separate
me from myself.

cube after cube
you dilute me so
longing for a mellower finish
rather than savor my bite at your throat.

say what you will
i will never be recognized
as something greater
than my components.

break me down
once you believe my impurities
have been removed
only the distilled spirit within me

will remain.

mafia

a broken life
is a made thing

once in it
there's no getting out.

blanched

life has bleached you
left you to desiccate
among the living, the proud
the unfeeling

the arms that hug you
become your chains
still you seek no freedom
only flee deeper within yourself

all your luster has been scalded
your eyes blanched by the thought
of truth

you will find no solace
like you will find no sun

god, i admire your beauty
so resolute in darkness
so absolute in the absence of love.

175

bane

we savored our only connection
these sins corked without repentance before us
i remember when you stole stars from my sky
but you laughed:

you're so over the moon

the turpentine an easy liquid to digest then;
it kept pretenses stripped clean

one september, you whispered:

how much lovelier we would be if dead

so i orchestrated a hymn for our funeral;
you fashioned wind chimes for our grave

now we dance slowly
the carillons a gentle ringing in our ears
this was the way it should have been for us;
that amber reflection in your eye
never more beautiful.

drowning cubes

he's angry
drowning cubes
in his glass
holding them without mercy
beneath the surface of the booze

clarity sobers him;
he asks for stirrers
more and more stirrers
and gets back to killing.

roadmap through a charred heart

you're holding a wonderful piece of artistry
a roadmap through a charred heart;
never allow it to be broken
set it ablaze instead

fuck the investigators
those pointing fingers toward arson;
if only they could be so brave

these are ashes
meticulously pieced together
not by love
while love may make you do crazy things
pain gets the job done

don't step carefully
stomp your foot down
there's nothing left to echo anyway
except the ghosts

gods write symphonies
men write tragedies
people like me just live the lie

once you close this artistry
i will be to you what i always have been
smudged.

about the author

Joseph A. Pinto is the author of the poetry collections *Scotch and Scars* (2020) and *A Distilled Spirit (2018)*, the poignant novella *Dusk and Summer (2014)* and the horror novel *Flowers for Evelene (2005)* - as well numerous dark fiction tales; his unique voice has been showcased in a multitude of anthologies and magazines as well as individually published short stories.

He is known as the barflypoet – and yes, he really writes his poetry from inside bars.

Indulge in Joseph's work at www.josephpinto.com

Follow him on Twitter: @JosephAPinto

Follow him on Instagram: @joseph_a_pinto

Follow him on Facebook as Joseph A. Pinto, barfly poet & author of dark fiction.

www.ingramcontent.com/pod-product-compliance
Lightning Source LLC
La Vergne TN
LVHW051051080426
835508LV00019B/1812